Saudade

Also by Traci Brimhall

POETRY
Our Lady of the Ruins
Rookery

FOR CHILDREN
Sophia & The Boy Who Fell (with Sarah Nguyen)

Saudade

Traci Brimhall

Copper Canyon Press
Port Townsend, Washington

Cover art: Papy and Milouz TSF Crew, *L'arbre*, 2013

Copper Canyon Press is in residence at Fort Worden State Park in Port Townsend, Washington, under the auspices of Centrum. Centrum is a gathering place for artists and creative thinkers from around the world, students of all ages and backgrounds, and audiences seeking extraordinary cultural enrichment.

LIBRARY OF CONGRESS CATALOGING-IN-PUBLICATION DATA
Names: Brimhall, Traci, 1982– author.
Title: Saudade / Traci Brimhall.
Description: Port Townsend, Washington : Copper Canyon Press, [2017]
Identifiers: LCCN 2017013439 | ISBN 9781556595172 (paperback : alk. paper)
Classification: LCC PS3602.R53177 A6 2017 | DDC 811/.6—dc23
LC record available at https://lccn.loc.gov/2017013439

9 8 7 6 5 4 3 2 FIRST PRINTING

Copper Canyon Press
Post Office Box 271
Port Townsend, Washington 98368

www.coppercanyonpress.org

para minha mãe

PURAQUEQUARA, 1953–TAMPA, 2014

ACKNOWLEDGMENTS

Many thanks to the editors of the following publications where these poems first appeared, sometimes in earlier versions:

Barn Owl Review, The Believer, Bellingham Review, Beloit Poetry Journal, Blackbird, Boston Review, Columbia Poetry Review, Connotation Press, Court Green, Crab Orchard Review, Crazyhorse, Fairy Tale Review, Four Way Review, Greensboro Review, Gulf Coast, Hayden's Ferry Review, Indiana Review, Kenyon Review, New England Review, New Republic, Oxford American, The Paris-American, Passages North, Pleiades, Ploughshares, Poet Lore, Poetry Northwest, Prairie Schooner, The Rumpus, Slate, Sonora Review, Southern Indiana Review, Spoon River Poetry Review, Subtropics, 32 Poems, Vinyl, Virginia Quarterly Review, Waxwing.

"After the Flood the Captain of the *Hamadryas* Discovers a Madonna" won *Passages North*'s Just Desserts Short-Short Fiction Prize, selected by Roxane Gay.

"Better to Marry Than to Burn" appeared in *Poetry*.

"In Which the Chorus Explains What Was Stolen in 1966" appeared in an earlier form, titled "Stolen, 1966," in *The New Yorker*.

"The Last Known Sighting of the Mapinguari," "Rapture: *Lucus*," and "What They Found in the Diving Bell" appeared in the Academy of American Poets Poem-a-Day Series.

"To Survive the Revolution" was selected by Terrance Hayes for *The Best American Poetry 2014*.

I'm so very grateful for the financial support provided by a National Endowment for the Arts Fellowship, a King-Chávez-Parks Fellowship, and the University of Mississippi's Summer Poet-in-Residence program, which allowed me to complete many of these poems.

I'm also deeply indebted to the support I received from faculty and students in Western Michigan University's English Department, especially Nancy Eimers, Elizabyth Hiscox, Krystal Howard, William Olsen, and Daneen Wardrop.

There were many people who helped greatly with the poems, but Natalie Diaz, Claudia Cortese, Sandra Beasley, Ali Barna, Tomás Q. Morín, and Lucy Biederman saw the manuscript as a whole and gave invaluable advice. My friends Brynn Saito and Lisa Fay Coutley kept me writing, even when it wasn't fun or convenient.

To Melissa da Silvera Serpa, Amy Sayre Baptista, and Paula Nieves, thank you for reigniting my interest in the past.

And for my mother, whose stories ended too soon and were never finished and are where I begin everything.

Saudade, or longing, is the desire to be transported from
        darkness into light,
to be touched by the hand of that which is not of this world.

Nick Cave, "The Secret Life of the Love Song"

Though they die of nostalgia, they'll never return.

Eduardo Galeano, *The Book of Embraces*

Contents

3   The Last Time I Saw My Daughter's Eyes, They Were on the Back of a Moth's Wings

MARIA JOSÉ

7   The Last Known Sighting of the Mapinguari

8   The Unconfirmed Miracles at Puraquequara

10   To Survive the Revolution

11   In Which the Chorus Describes Cafuné on the Eve of the Passion

13   Beg, Borrow, Steal

14   Seven Guesses

15   A Camera Crew Films a Telenovela Based on the Miracles at Puraquequara

16   In Which the Chorus Explains What Was Stolen in 1966

18   After the Plantation Fire

19   How I Lost Seven Faiths

20   In My Third Trimester I Dream My Own Death

21   In Which the Chorus Provides a Possible Chronology

THOMAS

25   Better to Marry Than to Burn

26   Atonement

28   Incomplete Address to the Lord

29   For the Glory

30   In Which the Chorus Proposes Performing Nebuchadnezzar's Dreams Instead of the Passion

32   Peace Be with Us

34   After Waking from a Seven-Year Dream

35   In Which the Chorus Sees an incomplete Vision of the Future

37 Sanctuary

38 Puerperal Fever

39 Overdue Epithalamium

40 And Again I Say Rejoice

41 In Which the Chorus Acts Out What May Be a Love Story

MARIA JOSÉ

47 After the Boto's Autopsy Reveals a Nautilus Where the Heart Should Be

48 Sacrament

49 In Which the Chorus Laments the Death of the Last Encantado

51 An Incomplete Memory of the Body

52 To Reduce Your Likelihood of Seduction by the Boto

54 The Fate of My Seven Husbands

56 If Marriage Is a Duel at Ten Paces

57 Belated Epithalamium

58 When I Go to Prison to Meet My Father

59 The Fate of My Seven Dolls

61 At Play in the Fields of the Lord

62 In Which the Chorus Paints a Family Portrait at Boi Bumbá

64 Revenant

65 What They Found in the Diving Bell

SOPHIA

69 Rapture: *Lucus*

70 *Ecce Homo,* He Says, and I Do

72 What We Lost in the Flood —

73 In Which the Chorus Appears at the Wedding Rehearsal, Ominous as Angels

75 Virago

77 On the Feast Day of Our Lady Hippolyta

79 The Heart in Jeopardy Fabricates a New Fortune

81 Reluctant Fugue

82 In Which the Chorus Whispers the Rumors

84 The Unverifiable Resurrection of Adão da Barco

85 After the Flood the Captain of the *Hamadryas* Discovers
a Madonna

87 Misbegotten

DON ANTONIO

91 Sibylline Translation

92 Plantation Landscape with Seven Unwanted Children and
Pollinating Rubber Trees

93 Il dolce suono

94 Translation Theory

95 Matar as Saudades

96 Belterra Exodus

97 After Seven Lullabies Vanish from the Library

98 In Which the Chorus Relates the Somewhat True History
of Puraquequara

100 The Hunger River

101 Idyll, or Impossible Epithalamium

102 In Which the Chorus Tries to Be as Clear as Possible

MARIA JOSÉ

107 Saudade

About the Author   *109*

Saudade

The Last Time I Saw My Daughter's Eyes,
They Were on the Back of a Moth's Wings

I'm almost ready to give her up for dead. I tried
believing she'll appear someday on a boat from
downriver where she's been making a living

as a dancer who glues yellow feathers to her breasts
and lets tourists eat maracujá from her navel.
I tried the easier faith of a gift-bearing God who

serves the whim of prayer, but all I got was this
ambitious hope, this heart that hangs upside down
in my ribs, blind and nocturnal and a glutton for fruit.

In a past life, I drowned with a rattlesnake wrapped
around my ankle. In another one, I danced for
a father's obedience. In this one, I throw a rope over

a ceiling beam and let it dangle over my bed. Its abiding
creak rocks me to sleep where John the Baptist comes
for me with a basilisk on his shoulders, calls me

by my maiden name, and says: *You have been weighed
and measured and found wanting stilettos and a lipstick
named Prima Donna.* It's not true, I try to say,

but each letter carves itself into a tree and holds
its blackness like a mirror. I see myself in every word,
only younger. I wake as libidinous and sincere

as Caruso in the morning lamenting his lost horse
on a Victrola. The rope above my bed is gone
and John the Baptist's head sits on my chest

like a wish seeking entrance to a well. *Where is she?*
I ask, turning his head over in my hands three times.
He opens his mouth to let down the flood.

Maria José

ALEGRIA

The Last Known Sighting of the Mapinguari

Before she died, my mother told me
I'd make the monster that would kill me,
but what crawled toward me was not

my lost daughter manifesting as myth —
this was someone else's death creeping
through my field, butchering my cow.

I recognized its lone eye and two mouths.
Perhaps it mistook the lowing for the call
of its own kind. I didn't mind the heifer,

but her calf circled, refusing to leave even
as the creature pulled out its mother's tongue,
fed one of its mouths and moaned

from the other. The intestines glowed
dully in the moonlight. The calf bawled.
The disappointed mapinguari sat,

thousands of worms rising from the split
heart it held, testing the strange night air.
I've outlived all the miracles that came for me.

My mother was wrong and not wrong,
like the calf who approached the monster
and licked the blood from its fingers.

The Unconfirmed Miracles at Puraquequara

First came reports of a leprous child who touched
the shrunken hand and was healed. A barren
woman pressed it to her womb and conceived.

Other claims followed — a manioc crop flourished
when a farmer danced the hand over his field,
a priest cast out a possessed boy's demon when

he used a finger to make the sign of the cross
on the boy's body. Whenever a believer paraded it
down church aisles, the square holes in Christ's wrists

closed. The man who discovered the shrunken fist
in the mouth of a dead jaguar said his manhood
doubled in size. I knew where it had come from,

this message that my daughter's body was still alive
and surely growing, but I said nothing. The town
had waited so long for a miracle, and it was finally

here, enriching the poor, emboldening the meek,
carving acrostic mysteries into the trees. So when
I caught it trying to escape the reliquary, I thought

I had no choice but to leash it to the altar. That's when
the manioc crop molded and the woman delivered
a stillbirth with flippers for feet and eyes

like small black planets. Demons returned to the boy.
He shook so hard he struck his head on a rock and died.
When the hunter went mad and strangled his wife, the whole

town was relieved. We knew what to do. We paraded him
to the city square where he wept — *Where's my wife?* —
as the priest prayed — *Deliver us* — and we all shouted —

Thief! — until his body stopped swaying and we cut
off his hands. Startled pigeons roosting on the church
roof took flight when they heard the clapping.

To Survive the Revolution

I, too, love the devil. He comes to my bed
all wrath and blessing and, wearing
my husband's beard, whispers, *Tell me who*

you suspect. He fools me the same way every time,
but never punishes me the same way twice.
I don't remember who I give him but he says

I have the instinct for red. Kiss red. Pleasure red.
Red of the ripe guaraná, of the jaguar's eyes
when it stalks the village at night. Red as the child

I birthed that my husband buried without me.
The stump of flesh where the head should be,
red. Pierced side of a disappointing Christ, red.

A sinner needs her sin, and mine is beloved.
Mine returns with skin under his fingernails,
an ice cube on his tongue, and covers my face

with a hymnal. I never ask for a miracle,
only strength enough to bear his weight.
Each day, I hang laundry on the line, dodge

every shadow. Each night he crawls
through the window, I pay with a name.
The God I don't believe in saves me anyway.

In Which the Chorus Describes Cafuné
on the Eve of the Passion

MARIA HELENA

The night in costumes, in church bells, in pews sucking on free
salted caramels.

MARIA THEREZA

In the general's breath before he pinches the child's jaw open and
spits in her mouth.

MARIA HELENA

We did nothing to stop it. Why would we? We only witness, record,
recite.

MARIA THEREZA

Besides, no one else tried to stop history from bringing itself to
the stage. Everyone fantasized a different present.

MARIA DE LOURDES

In the pews, the unrepentant traced their hands onto hymnal
pages. Behind the curtain, the toothless, the leprous, burying
themselves in scherzos and nude boas.

MARIA THEREZA

Jesus makes it onstage but forgets his lines, the new Passion sim-
mers in the journalist, the priest, the poet, watching the dictator's
parade from an unlit room, composing meager epics and running
the planchette across the letters written on the wall:

MARIA MADALENA

Will we survive?

MARIA APARECIDA

Of course not.

MARIA MADALENA

Will the country?

MARIA APARECIDA

Ask again later.

MARIA MADALENA

Is God's love absolute?

MARIA APARECIDA

Nana, nenê.

MARIA DE LOURDES

The night is ripping its dress to bind soldiers' wounds. It's painting the church with the blood on the torturer's floor.

MARIA HELENA

It's nailing together the gallows.

MARIA THEREZA

It's combing men's hair with its fingers, singing, *o nenê dorme no chão,* and measuring their necks.

Beg, Borrow, Steal

They fingerprint the severed left hand
at the police station and all the officers
start carrying prostheses in their pockets

in case they discover my daughter alive
but handless. Everyone makes a spare —
the carpenter whittles one, the dressmaker

stitches one, the coroner pickles one
and experiments with electricity and leeches.
All of us plant offerings to lure her home —

tattered bassinet, puppet theater in a mannequin's
hollowed chest, a suit of armor posed midstride
as though some uncanny conquistador resurrected

himself and continued his search for El Dorado.
I plaster walls with pictureless posters — *MISSING:*
my reason for living. Last seen: pink as life and wailing.

Tourists return from their searches shouting
premeditated epiphanies, claiming they found proof
of life and the postscript of a ransom note requesting

old opera records, or else. My tongue inside the licked
envelope, detective and clue. I barter for what
remains of her, ignore the warning in the first half

of the ransom — *All action leads to suffering. So does all hope.*
At dawn I find not my daughter, not her other hand,
but a word as light as terror parting the trees.

Seven Guesses

My daughter is dead or being raised by a jamboree of jaguars
with her dress pulled over her head, pretending to be the ghost
of a blind king, or my husband will bring her body back from

where he hid it and parade her on the back of a white-eyed mule,
or she turned into a dolphin like her father and followed him
to the Orinoco where his bedtime stories feature laundry, jacaranda

blossoms, and a lovely hunchback with seven fetishes – collars, corsets,
cuffs, scratches, spankings, strap-ons, and dolls in leather shoes –
or my daughter is the tree-shaped tumor in my skull, or the echo

of a lullaby, all lonesome song and no body, or she's a character
in the book authored by my inner voice, the one where my mother
is limping but alive, and my father escapes from prison,

and we eat guaraná grown from the left eye of the boy
whose grave opened to greet his weeping mother and a forest
rushed out, a child's eye ripening in the mouth of every bird.

A Camera Crew Films a Telenovela Based
on the Miracles at Puraquequara

I rehearse my lines as I palm a maracujá to test its tenderness
and say, *Não, Comandante,* and, *More rum, cadela.* Day in, day out,
I eat the same fried bread and ripe plantains, wash the same sheets,

keep saving the saved, the baptized rising from the river,
awed and dripping, living their scripts. Though my memory
of the execution differs I stand on my mark and clap.

I try to recall my insincere lamentations in the funeral parade.
An extra in my own story and envious of the ingenue's unmuddied
shoes and air-conditioned hotel room, I say, *Ajudar, ajudar,*

and cry on cue. Between scenes an actor shares imported cigars
with the prostitute playing me. When cameras roll, he bites
her nipples with his prosthetic teeth, and my milk lets down.

Sweet white ache. After the mayor hangs himself and bequeaths
his second-best bed to his horse, I write romantic obituaries
and send his wife signed photographs of myself. I make love

to avoid sweeping the sidewalk, to practice geometry, to satisfy
the voyeur and come with uncertain pleasure. Only when the film crew
leaves do the dead reappear, drinking, dancing, whipping each other

with TV antennas. They burn with more heat than light.
Pictures from that night reveal a black horse dragging a priest
through paradise, the crowd weeping, at last, with happiness.

In Which the Chorus Explains What Was Stolen in 1966

MARIA DE LOURDES

One candidate swore he'd import artists from Paris to paint every voter's portrait.

MARIA HELENA

But the wiretap revealed that of the six masked balls and two bull-fights he promised, he only planned to pass out free twelve-packs of Guaraná Antarctica on election day.

MARIA APARECIDA

One candidate skipped town when someone caught him digging up a body and reburying it beneath the courthouse.

MARIA THEREZA

Another rumor said he was caught tattooing women after curfew, inking diabolical love letters onto their ankles.

MARIA MADALENA

He was part of a conspiracy of windmills, others claimed.

MARIA DE LOURDES

They said his chickens accused him of unspeakable things.

MARIA HELENA

When we arrived to cast our ballots, the soldiers at the polls handed us a picture of the general leading the charge against the Bolivian army and a picture of the president's house stormed by sailors.

MARIA APARECIDA

We all voted for the general twice, the dim X of our voice. We went to the town square, and danced with short men with long mus-taches who buried their bristled cheeks in our chests and swore to help you when the borders open if we'd only let them sign their names on our thighs.

MARIA THEREZA

We tried to tell them, we did. We were born a century before them and will last centuries after. This was not a fear to run from. We liked it, their acrid sweat, their promises of a future.

MARIA MADALENA

One planned our escape in a canoe under a dead fisherman.

MARIA DE LOURDES

One said he'd pack us in a sack when he shipped his manioc.

MARIA APARECIDA

One promised to write us a poem whose music would transport us over the Andes, even if our bodies remained here.

MARIA THEREZA

My brides, said the first, offering a hook.

MARIA MADALENA

Beloveds, said the second, holding a rose.

MARIA DE LOURDES

Muses, wrote the third, slipping notes in each of our pockets.

MARIA HELENA

We chose.

After the Plantation Fire

We buried the bodies and danced—we had to.
Beneath the sagging porch, generators roared,
mosquitoes sated themselves on wild dogs, boats

approaching on the river loaded with soldiers
killed their engines. We told them the fire had nothing
to do with the revolution. I've made the choice

between brushing flies from a child's eyes or digging
a grave deeper. It's easier than you'd think. So what
if I knew who he was when he sidled close—

hat tilted back, caipirinha in his hand—and matched
his hips with mine? I toyed with his buttons, felt scars
through his shirt. I didn't tell him where our daughter

had gone or what my husband had done. He kissed
the blood blisters on my fingertips and never asked
how I got them. That's not why he'd come.

When soldiers broke the lights and the musicians' arms,
I brought him to the burned plantation, hid his face beneath
my skirt and leaned against a rubber tree—still alive

and leaking sap. Somewhere in the new dark, a man
in a uniform cut off another man's tongue and ordered him
to sing. Wind pushed the flames closer to heaven.

How I Lost Seven Faiths

I was given my first god as a child, a side-speared redeemer
who rose and walked after death but whose broken body
hung over his transubstantiated blood. When my daughter

vanished, I adopted a book of spells in a foreign tongue.
When my homophonic translations of curses didn't give me
my daughter back or even a sign, I tried the rabbi who lived

in his tomb twenty-three hours a day and came out at noon
to eat hummingbird tongues served in mango compote
and honey. After my rabbinical miracle wore off I tried

divination by umbrellas and solar devotion but gave them up
for the euphoric theology of handling snakes. I lost faith in that,
too, when I woke to a constrictor choking on my big toe.

My undisciplined doubt didn't sharpen my questions or make
the harem of angels stop haunting my godless mind. *Better,*
people said. *It would get better.* But I didn't want better.

I wanted my daughter back. I wanted to live back
in the before. Before love possessed me. Before grief.
Someone left a black cryptorchid goat in my yard. I fed it

coconut milk and Communion wine, brushed its coat, crooning,
Remember me when you come into your kingdom. From that day on
my silvering hair darkened, my tumor shrank to a seed.

I aged back to twenty, to ten, to two. People brought me
hot chocolate and asked to be blessed, but I was shrinking
and prelingual, so possible, so small, so brightened by sound.

In My Third Trimester I Dream My Own Death

In week twenty-seven, I dream a conquistador
confronts me with unsigned Requerimientos.
I'd give up any god to save a life, so I sign

them all with a narwhal tooth dipped in squid ink.
I bring a scalpel with me in week thirty in case I meet
my husband in my dreams asking again, again, *Whose*

child is this? Whose child? Oracular tremblings wake me
in warm sweats after a thief who speaks in vowels warns
I will resort to prayer in week thirty-three. His body

shines with the cruel radiance of a man who buried
himself alive and returned to laugh, dance, pick cupuaçu.
Jubilate. Week forty I spy rogue angels, jealous

of their god's fertile will, impregnating virgin orchids
in the rain forest. They promise to trade the ecstasies
of the anther cap for my firstborn daughter and before

I can say no, I wake to my water broken, my dreams
crawling out of the river, maculate and toothed,
insisting, *Even before you imagined us, we knew you.*

In Which the Chorus Provides a Possible Chronology

MARIA DE LOURDES

History began but did not write itself.

MARIA MADALENA

Language, or at least a word.

MARIA APARECIDA

War. Famine. Plague. Birth. Another war. Weddings. A country is called discovered by another country, the people called converts. Sapphires. Sugarcane. Rubies. In 1879, rubber.

MARIA HELENA

An opera house in the jungle. The age of the rubber baron. Desire begets money begets happiness begets desire begets an affair between an opera singer and a rubber baron.

MARIA THEREZA

Then yellow fever. Then rubber seeds smuggled out. Then villas burn.

MARIA DE LOURDES

1918, those who are left make towns out of bends in the river. Capitalists build rubber plantations. An island becomes a leper colony.

MARIA MADALENA

Date unknown: Freedom begets too much idle love. A boto arrives and begins to sing his pink song to town daughters.

MARIA APARECIDA

Time passes marked by floods and all the children born of the boto are named Maria.

MARIA HELENA

Then an American missionary comes to town with three crates: Bibles, medicine, and food. He is two-thirds beloved.

MARIA THEREZA

1964, coup d'état. Disappearances, death, torture, death, etc.

MARIA DE LOURDES

And then a child's hand is found in a jaguar's mouth. It belongs to a missing girl/a leper/is God's gangrenous stump. Miracles arrive whether they are welcome or not.

MARIA MADALENA

Unknown, the date of the plantation fire. Caused by arson/lightning/the amputated hand. Miracles stop or they never happened at all.

MARIA APARECIDA

1972, the town of Puraquequara vanishes and rises again.

MARIA DE LOURDES

All the children flee and begin to sing for their supper in Manaus. We sing of a boto, of miracles, of the hand that gave and took away. We sing fire. We sing flood. We sing the word carved into rubber trees. We sing for the childhoods they never had and the childhoods they did. We sing history in reverse so the story might end in birth.

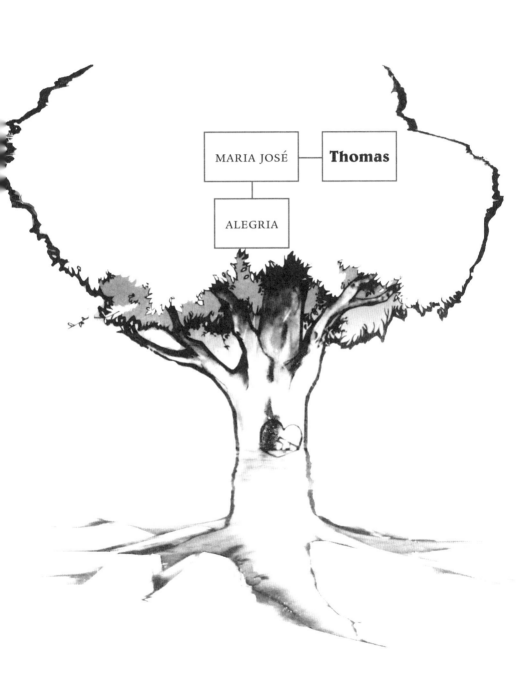

Better to Marry Than to Burn

Home, then, where the past was.
Then, where cold pastorals repeated
their entreaties, where a portrait of Christ
hung in every bedroom. Then was a different
country in a different climate in a time when
souls were won and lost in prairie tents.
Then it was a dream. I had no will there.
Then the new continent and the new wife
and the new language for no, for unsaved,
for Communion on credit. Then the daughter
who should've been mine, and the hour a shadow
outgrew its body. Then the knowledge of God
like an apple in the mouth. I faced my temptation.
I touched its breasts with as much restraint
as my need allowed, and I woke with its left hand
traced again and again on my chest with mud
like a cave wall disfigured. It was holy.
It was fading. My ring, then, on my finger
like an ambush, as alive as fire. Then the trees
offered me a city in the shape of a word.
Then a choir filed out of the jungle singing
hallelujah like a victory march and it was.

Atonement

I chose my death on a black day in June
when rain came in sideways from the windows
and my wife lay unmoving on the floor.
I'd lived for three years in my silence,
the faithful beseeching my dumb mouth
for a revelation. *Heaven is cheap!* I wrote
across the book of Luke. *All God wants*
is for you to think of loaves and fish when you dance.
I don't blame anyone for leaving me except
my wife. Her hips used to charm the reais
out of a man's pockets, but now she sleeps
with the cows and when she brings me
coffee – black, sweet, and steaming –
she smells like piss. Maybe I tried to teach her
a lesson, but I never meant the pain to last.
To ask her forgiveness, I snuck onto the plantation
and astonished a rubber tree, reopening
its cuts and collecting its sap in my hands.
I wanted to shape it into a heart but it pooled
into moonlight, it rolled into a ball, it tried
to become a kite but became a burning book.
I knelt before it and whispered, *Show me my enemy,*
and I will sew her lips shut until she submits
or unmakes the world. When I went home, my wife
told me someone set fire to the plantation.
Everyone would starve this season. I tried to make her
hold still so I could pierce her lips with a needle.
God loves you, I said and finally believed it.
She kissed me with her bloodied mouth
and went to feed the cows. I painted my lips

with sap and went to save the trees.
My God, I said, and the fire said, *Yes.*

Incomplete Address to the Lord

When I found that mass of scales and muscle,
saw one anaconda twist around another, watched
a split tongue flick the air, choosing me, black
as the devil's own and twice as thick, males coiled
around the female tickling her back with their spurs,
I knew I'd give anything to be her. I felt the pulse
in my eyelid, tasted the ants that paraded over
my plantains at night, drank all the darkness out
of my wife's breast. Lord, I'd rather be crazy
than broken. The city bore its own children who
crawled from the gutters, their eyes in their pockets
and lepers' ashes in their mouths. They don't believe
you exist even though they wrap slices of lamb
in the pages of the book you wrote for the illiterate
shepherds. I know you know this. You with your name
on the lips of graceless women. You with your face
tattooed on men's arms. You who weep fire but never
for the dead. My Lord, I admit it. I let the angel win.
He wrapped himself around me, pinned me
to the riverbed, and I rose up wet, reeking, wearing
my shadow like a dress. When I pressed my chest,
milk bled a halo into the water. For an hour I was whole,
my heart undressed itself. Temptation wore me down
to my socks and assembled me back into my old body.
I'm still the man you made in the image of who
you used to be, my lover turned back into my rib,
and you who gifted me with a second skin,
I don't want your inch of flesh. I want everyone
who comes looking for me to find —

For the Glory

When my wife's unbaptized body begins to swell,
I see the sin that should've been mine has been offered
to someone else. O ruin. O want. I taunt the baby
when it's born, swear I will make it know its truth.
I take it to the jungle, dig a hole and set it in its grave.
O awful fruit. It smiles at me with pointed teeth,
so I let it live. Sometimes I tell myself I stay
in the jungle for the glory of God, even though
I've never converted anyone. I tell my wife
her daughter is dead but return to hum hymns
to the black-eyed girl and feed her raw fish and milk.
I sing for the glory, write sermons for the glory,
resist my wife's sinful flesh for the glory, O unbearable rib.
One night, I forget to cover the hole, and a jaguar
eats the girl's left hand. Binding the stump at her wrist,
I touch the tender points of her new breasts with my thumbs.
O heavenly dark rendered in a woman's body. I wake
and find the grave empty. My wife says she is ready
to serve a god instead of a man. It isn't easier,
but it will die for you more happily. O ungovernable
blood. She hears gossip about a wild girl thieving
from fishermen's nets. She lies for the story,
does time for the story, prefers the rumor
to the truth. It promises the dead make a new life
carving elegies into trees. Not a god's afterlife
but a daughter's. The butterfly she buries returns
three days later as a word engraved on a strangler fig.
O miracle. O mystery. O hopeful stab of joy.

In Which the Chorus Proposes Performing
Nebuchadnezzar's Dreams instead of the Passion

MARIA MADALENA

Why all this resurrection? Why all this whipping and crowning
and crying to the heavens? Why not the Hanging Gardens instead
of Gethsemane?

MARIA THEREZA

Why not a statue of gold and clay, why not a tree cut down, why
not a prophecy and its interpreter instead of angels chaperoning
a resurrection?

MARIA DE LOURDES

Why not live in the wild for seven years, humbled, an animal, sin-
less and closer to God instead of in a tomb for three days, waiting
backstage for God to sublime your soul back to Earth?

MARIA HELENA

Why not monomania, porphyria, a lycanthropic delusion of his-
torical proportions?

MARIA APARECIDA

Forget the burden of eternity, this is such a good moon for
howling.

MARIA MADALENA

Forget Barabbas was ever a choice. Forget Mary trying to cradle
the weight of her dead son's body and let's move on to the ban-
quet of Belshazzar.

MARIA THEREZA

Let's skip forever and feast on now. Let's drink from the stolen
cups before God's hand graffities our walls, before night falls on

the king, before Daniel is sentenced to feverish prayer.

MARIA DE LOURDES

Let's pick up the palm fronds and set free the lambs.

MARIA HELENA

Let the lions wait for the bodies of our enemies.

Peace Be with Us

That was the year the chickens drowned in the flood,
the year I dreamed of empty coffins and went mute,
when the bodies washing up on the riverbank
with burned soles and welted backs were called suicides,
and no one told the children any different.
They wanted to throw the ruined hens off the dock
to see if piranhas would eat them. Everyone thinks
that's the day I stopped speaking, but I understood
that children grow excited when they're hungry
and new to cruelty. I washed the lice from their hair
with kerosene and killed the jaguar that returned
from the jungle with the wild girl's hand in its mouth.
She vanished like a new moon, but I dreamed
she was shot by soldiers and only I could hear her
pounding inside a coffin. But when I lifted the lid,
I found another, smaller coffin, and another, and another,
until it was so small I couldn't pry it open, but I heard
her weeping, and I couldn't stop the knocking, so I swallowed it.
When the children buried the dogs, they blamed me
for their wildness, so I let them toss the chickens
into the river, thinking the dead don't mind
what becomes of them. I could absolve them later.
I watched what they did — saw their faces brighten
when the water came alive. Some days God requires
too much of us. It wasn't until the next day after pulling
another body with blackened feet out of the river
that I was struck dumb. I couldn't help myself.
I found a hole in the corpse's throat and thought
There. The coffin is there, and this time I can open it.
The body didn't turn toward me when I pushed
my finger in and pulled out a wet curl of down.

I opened its mouth and saw white feathers.
Dozens of them. This was the world
I was commanded to love.

After Waking from a Seven-Year Dream

It comes in my sleep and then it comes up the river,
a tiger shark with its young in its mouth all singing
the same commandment — *Thou shalt kiss thy mistress's
Song of Solomon thighs and belly and the star tattoo
on her left areola.* I kiss the pear hanging between
her breasts and every link of the chain that holds
it there. I kiss ghosts in her ears, the ones who
whisper as she enters sleep, that last wilderness,
to escape my wrathful appetites. I tongue
the pillowcase, nibble the headboard, laugh
as I take each pair of panties from her drawer
and treat them to the most abiding pleasures.
I worship the shark until I'm no longer afraid of it,
pull out its teeth, carve my name into confessionals
and bathroom stalls. I kiss the teeth. I kiss my name.
I kiss every woman who accepts my last dream
as payment. I kiss doorknobs and empty soda bottles,
trap thunder in my mouth and give it to every child
I can catch. We who are about to see God's wet hair.
We who are about to bind ourselves to trees. I lick
cobwebs beneath the saint's skirt, kiss his legs free
of dust, slander his mortality with my tongue until
I come into the godscape, blind and spitting live flies.

In Which the Chorus Sees an Incomplete Vision of the Future

MARIA HELENA

And in fourteen years, six days, and two hours, a solstice.

MARIA DE LOURDES

And in the guerrilla's pocket, a pacemaker for the dictator.

MARIA APARECIDA

And on a girl's necklace, a wedding ring pulled from a dead hand.

MARIA THEREZA

And on the docks, our abandoned dresses, whitening in the sun.

MARIA MADALENA

And in the mother's purse, a bloody fish in last century's newspaper.

MARIA HELENA

And on the father's lap, a napkin and stolen underwear.

MARIA DE LOURDES

And on his bookshelf, the decoded cryptolex, unread, and on his bedside table, a plastic comb with a missing girl's hair in the teeth, and in his sock drawer, a firework that, when lit, becomes the face of Carmen Miranda, all smile and chica chica boom chic.

MARIA APARECIDA

And in the river, our skin changing, pinkening at last.

MARIA THEREZA

And in the grave, an answer, waiting.

MARIA MADALENA

And in the streetlamp, two witch moths mating.

MARIA HELENA

And in the trees, a sloth. And in the trees, a mother capuchin picking lice from her baby's fur. And on the trees, a word, writing itself.

MARIA DE LOURDES

And below the trees, the penultimate sinkhole.

MARIA APARECIDA

And above the trees, a star seeking Omega, a bright zero, a pulsing no.

Sanctuary

There's only one place God cannot find me.
God with his hooves on, God with his horns
come to force me back to my knees with his love.
Fear abandons me at the sight of her with a black wig
and a belt in her hand. She knows the body's ambition
to be all sweat and flush and rapture. She paints
a mustache on my upper lip and offers me moth wings
instead of the Eucharist, which wouldn't save me anyway,
but I wanted a small measure of penitence to make
my knees go numb. This love did not, in fact,
redeem me, but it did take my toes in its mouth
and call me by pleasure's other name. I was happy then,
all bristle and bruised wrists, licking a stranger's sweat
from my wife's breast, saturnine and weeping over
the gospels in my pocket. I understood my sorrow
over the world does not change it. My horror couldn't
unbury the bodies or make electrodes burn the torturer's
hands instead. Better this choice to be powerless,
enthralled, to forgive God's ambition to be free of us.

Puerperal Fever

Don't believe what she says about me.
I bathed her breasts in rosewater and milk,
seawater and clay, whatever she did and did not
ask for, but never once put her in my mouth
to ease her. Why would I? I already knew too much
of the body's wet holiness. I hid her child
and waited for my second death to seek me.
I gave her the doll instead of her daughter
to see how she sorrowed, watched her rock
its bound lips to her left nipple. I wanted
to warn her, but I knew we must each live
according to our hungers. I watch her sleep
with her legs open, her mouth monstrous
in the grave light of morning. You can believe her
when she sings about the black heat of paradise.
I've been. Death found me in a rubber plantation
six days ago molesting a pitcher plant with
my adulterous tongue and middle finger. I rode
through hell on a burning horse but came back
to tell you every miracle wants something
in return. I reached through a slit in the black
curtain and felt the gates of heaven stitched shut.

Overdue Epithalamium

By the power vested in the anemic priest, I now
pronounce Paradise overthrown and offer you
the queen's heart I plucked from the garden
and a kiss. Come to my house where last night
I strangled a courteous succubus and buried her
embalmed with gold dust beneath the bed.
Unwrap sheets embroidered with twelve positions
of love I censored with scissors and model
the bent knees and arched back of consummation.
It is perverse and chaste and likely to be forgiven.
I write plagiarized erotica on your wedding gown
as you sleep, paint matching watercolor bruises
on your arms that you wash when waking, saying,
*Strengthen me with raisins, refresh me with apples, for I
am faint with love.* I give you my hand, my life,
my reluctant obedience. Promise me your death
and forever. Say you mean it. So help me God.

And Again I Say Rejoice

Time is measured twice – by flood and by plantation fire,
and I survived neither. I moved to this country after
they bombed the dictator's door and caught him in the act
of contrition, writing love letters to the Virgin Mary
with one hundred eight splinters in his fingers.
Graffiti says his spirit calcified and tumbled to earth as bone.
There's nothing left for a prisoner to do except rejoice.
In the time it takes the severed head to fall into the waiting
basket, a child steals reais left on a table, a sacaca turns into
a fish and back into a man, a fetus grows two new hairs.
If rumors are true, God loves nothing more than the unborn
and ripe guaraná. Underneath his robes, Jesus is all verb
and mustard seed. The Holy Ghost stops at every café to enjoy
the perverse taste of chocolate in strangers' mouths. I am
a God-fearing man. A bullet sings louder than I can. A guerrilla
prays faster. On another continent, I am known by my rapture.

In Which the Chorus Acts Out
What May Be a Love Story

MARIA DE LOURDES

Once there was a village of stunned lunatics who fingered their
navels as they stared at the moon's gray and abstinent seas.

MARIA MADALENA

Hard to believe we mean nothing to the stars.

MARIA APARECIDA

One day a nameless pink dolphin came to the village.

MARIA HELENA

His body a curse.

MARIA THEREZA

His beauty the least of it.

MARIA APARECIDA

His body as unsure of itself as a hypothesis.

MARIA DE LOURDES

One day he realized each child in the village was his, and he died
for them.

MARIA HELENA

And everyone wept.

MARIA THEREZA

And everyone gave his body to the tide's restless lisping.

MARIA APARECIDA

And every romance they repeated concealed a shame.

MARIA DE LOURDES

Once there was a daughter bewitched by the darkest lullaby pulled from a fairy-tale wet nurse.

MARIA MADALENA

In the refrain, a spell breaks and vowels heal around it.

MARIA APARECIDA

One day, a messenger was born in retrograde, ecstatic and sexless.

MARIA HELENA

She wandered like an angel curious about its source.

MARIA THEREZA

She wandered like a pilgrim smitten with wine.

MARIA APARECIDA

She wandered like orphans in search of a plantation to call an ending.

MARIA MADALENA

The message survived the flood. Then, the fire. Then even the jaguar let her live, and we knew she was ours to hunt, ours to worship or subdue.

MARIA THEREZA

One day, we loved what was easy – a grand piano half-drowned in the river, parakeets mating in a minor key, inventing history rather than recording it.

Now we love what is more beautiful than us, which is the weight-lessness of fire, which is the amputated girl learning to write with her left hand, which is light is terror is coming for us.

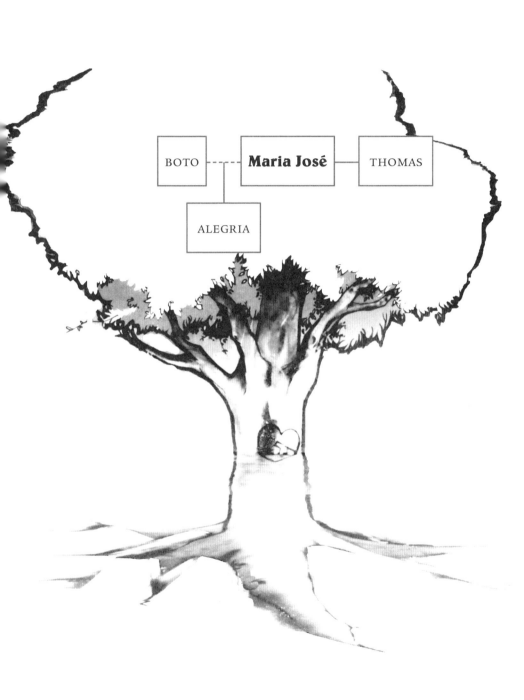

After the Boto's Autopsy Reveals a Nautilus
Where the Heart Should Be

The whirlpool gives back the past – pirate ship,
cartographer's notebook, the runaway nun,
an adoring cockatiel and his late mistress,

the chronicles of Orellana, who went in search of gold
and cinnamon and named the river – not for himself
but for the women who attacked him. A colony

can't disinherit the empire's sin. Ghosts keep crawling
off museum shelves and writing want ads – *Will share
secrets of underworld for food.* I'm a coward who prefers

the secular doom of devils who negotiate the terms
of our surrender. I want to go back further, before
the denouement, before the climax, to the action

rising beyond the river, past the dead lining the docks
like an inventory of loss. The whirlpool gives up
its history, the promises, the miracles, the stolen

kisses. When I rebury the skeletons in white dresses,
six sunburned virgins walk down the street carrying
toucan eggs wrapped in warped pages from

Song of Solomon, the love letters folded in dress pockets,
rolled in stockings, taped to the inside of their thighs,
more than we bargained for and not enough.

Sacrament

I shouldn't have done it, but I wanted, just once,
for those boys to fear me. They mocked my hunched back
for years, said it was as crooked as the devil's dick.

I've never met the devil, but I met his son. He crawled out
of the water at dusk, pressed jacarandas to my thighs,
told me to think about the day I disrobed the Virgin

to feel her indigo breasts, and my spine grew straight
as the flaming sword guarding Paradise. Her breasts
were veined like mine, Heaven's sinister blue

branching from heart to skin. The next time the boys
threw rocks at my hump, I showed myself to them,
upright and sinning, petals trembling between my legs.

There was no room in their crowded imagination
for a story like mine. Three weeks later, two drowned,
and one went blind. I brought Communion to his house.

His dumb white eyes stared up at me unstartled. His trust
was terrible to behold, his innocence monstrous. He took
the host into his mouth and my hand blushed with forgiveness.

In Which the Chorus Laments the Death
of the Last Encantado

MARIA DE LOURDES

Once the river had its fill of miracles, he washed up on shore and could no longer become a man.

MARIA THEREZA

He clicked and lifted his flukes but they wouldn't split into legs.

MARIA MADALENA

A ribereña recognized him by his sadness and the scars on his back, his nearly visible history.

MARIA HELENA

She touched the dolphin she'd made love to as a man when she was sixteen, shy, and full of disquiet.

MARIA APARECIDA

Years ago he'd knocked on her door selling novel wonders — lockets, apples, French kisses.

MARIA DE LOURDES

At her insistence, he pulled her dress to her hips and used his tongue to write untranslatable Sapphic gospels between her thighs.

MARIA THEREZA

Where do you think you're going? she asked. *To what home? Toward which family?* But his untransformed body didn't respond.

MARIA MADALENA

She walked the streets wailing and striking her calves with a bull-whip, announcing the death of the last encantado.

MARIA HELENA

As the clouds ripened, they went weeping to collect him, remembering the slow millennium of postcoital untwining, the water dripping from his hair baptizing their necks and navels and knees. The howler monkeys joined them with their ministry about pleasure and anger and fruit. The forest was alive with it, the story of the love they'd made. The love that made us.

MARIA APARECIDA

They placed him in a canoe with his hat and our kisses, lianas and imported apples, rosaries and fishhooks.

MARIA DE LOURDES

His love was as impersonal as it was perfect, and now it is the tide.

MARIA THEREZA

His body rocked toward a future we could not see.

MARIA MADALENA

The hollow he left in the riverbank swelled with rain.

An Incomplete Memory of the Body

I knew the rumors but sang the song anyway.
Sure enough, he came to me naked
with a dimple in his chin, one eye hooked

by a fisherman, hair still wet from the river.
He may or may not have cried the whole time
we made love with the same kind of puzzlement

I felt when I saw a girl in the streets of Manaus
carrying her own leash and a bowl for coins.
He smiled and one eye wept as he took

my fingers in his mouth. His spit made them itch
to touch his earlobes, his triceps, his elbows.
I can't recall a navel. There were or were not

scars on his back from boat propellers. I heard
my name shouted in the jungle, but none of my cries
were for help. I may or may not have felt the fin

start to rise from his spine before he ran
to the river. All the suspicious fires coming
toward me through the trees brightened.

To Reduce Your Likelihood of Seduction by the Boto

Do not swim. Do not swim in moonlight. Do not swim
naked in the moonlight. Do not swim in the floral bikini
you ordered from a catalogue. Do not walk too close to a river

or he may have his hand on your ass and call you *Sweetheart*
before you know it. He wants your legs wrapped around
his waist, though he may settle for your stroking his flippers

and tossing him fish. For now. But do not row your canoe
across the river. Do not row your canoe across the river
without a chaperone. Row your canoe across the river

with a chaperone who's been seduced before and knows
the warning signs of swooning. Do not fall for his wholesale
sadness. Cut your hair. Change your name. Do not accept

an invitation to dance from a hatted figure trying to pass
for a man. You're his type because he's never seen you before.
You must be new to town, or someone's wife. Do not sing

fados, even under your breath. Do not recite your soliloquy
about your fondness for deviant romance on the docks.
Do not think your fetish will turn him off. He's done

stranger things and with less pleasure. He needs consent
at every button, hook, zipper, and tie, but he has pornographic
lips and the patience of a thousand-year-old myth. Do not

imagine his favorite positions. Do not imagine his favorite
positions are the same as yours. Do not imagine him kissing
the cysts in your earlobes – he's imagining that right now.

Do not trust the dark advice of the leash. Though you have
the upper hand, he can't die until he collects the *yeses*
of every woman in town. Do not leave your front door

unlocked or he will arrive, quick as an angel at a virgin's
bedside, the coming so sudden it won't let go until
it receives your blessing, his release as easy as your *Please.*

The Fate of My Seven Husbands

My first husband went mute after I birthed another
man's child, set fire to the closest plantation, and when
his own fire couldn't kill him, I helped fake his death.

Everyone performed their grief until he couldn't bear
the stories and rose from his casket, stumbled into
the wild. My second husband left me at the cemetery

where I met the third, laying flowers on his victims' graves.
My fourth marriage was a knife I used to sever myself
from a Christ who never blessed me. I kept a clean pair

of underwear in my purse for the day he left me
for wanting to take what had already been given.
My fifth marriage, to a centaur with a roan body

and my first husband's face, took place in a dream,
a strange beguilement, a nightmare curling pink
at the edges. I woke to the general's sour breath

as he covered my face with a hymnal and brushed
my thigh with his dead wife's hair. God never gave
me a single usable passion, but did give me sharp teeth

and a strong jaw. I married the police captain leading
the search. Each night he came home with no news
of the missing and told me about graves unhoused, bodiless,

some new terror authored by the devil. The general
lived, he was sure, buried alive, subsisting on beetles
and storm water. When my seventh husband appeared

out of the jungle nursing a red-haired infant, weak milk
leaking from his nipples, skin cleaving to his ribs, every
shred of logic in me said, *Sweet doubter, you've returned.*

If Marriage Is a Duel at Ten Paces

Let's count our steps with endearments. *Honey. My love.*
Let's mix our gunpowder with rouge and foxglove seeds.
If marriage is a war for independence, I'll find a feather

for my cap and shoot you from your horse. *Darling doubter.*
If it's a hunt, salt and cure me. If it's a plague for two,
my dear, let's quarantine ourselves in the cemetery wearing

aprons and snakeskin belts. Let's disfigure each other
with praise. *My beautiful. My fugitive.* If monogamy is a stakeout,
sweetheart, let's spy on the beekeeper who lactates honey.

I'll pull stingers from your chest if you'll clean the blood
from under my nails. If romance is a ballad, we are its authors
and its victims and finished in four minutes. *Beloved,* if your

desire is the passage you underlined in Song of Solomon after
our first kiss and erased on our honeymoon, then dark am I,
yet lovely. Then you, *my shepherd, my charioteer,* turn and shoot.

Belated Epithalamium

I haven't written a love poem before now because I hoped
you'd notice the roasted snake served with cinnamon apples,
or see the dictionary of endearments I carved into the floors,

or realize I storyboarded our six weeks of love on the back
of your shirt. As long as the moon husbands the stars, I'll let
parishioners place coins in my open mouth as you pass me

down the aisles. I'll bolt jackalope busts to the bar wall.
I'll dress like a horse for you, harness for you, jingle and canter
for you, but I won't go to the river. I saw what waits there.

It's not a god but has a god inside it. Baptizing me in my sleep
doesn't count. We both know that. The malagueta bouquet
won't persuade me. The cilice crowning my thigh can't

convince me either. You carved crucifixes on my shoes,
mixed holy water in my shampoo before I realized you don't
know how much your vow will make us suffer, but I do.

When I Go to Prison to Meet My Father

they bring a Spaniard with a glass eye and tattooed fingers.
He holds my hands across the table and tells me the story
of Iara, Our Maritime Lady of Gunpowder Kisses, who sang

to sailors until a red tide strangled out a song about a myrmidon
with a forked tail, a rattle for a tongue. I don't tell the guard
this isn't my father but offer the prisoner consoling fictions

about kites I flew over Guanabara Bay, about black boots
embroidered with orchids I found on a rooster's grave.
I imagine love, and then I feel it. I admit to planting crosses

in termite mounds, not — as the priest declared — to blaspheme
the Lord but so they, too, might devour Christ and be saved.
He reopened the murdered woman's eyes, not — as the prosecution

claimed — to steal them but so she might be promoted to glory.
Police found the bloody knife wrapped in her slip, but not
her wallet, or her dress, or the letter she wrote her son in São Paulo.

There is a moral happiness in the incestuous bellbird's lure.
Its hunger comes to tell us of a world elsewhere. A body in need,
then a needless body roused to dream the everlasting alone.

The Fate of My Seven Dolls

They arrive from America the day of the funeral,
seams in their dresses unfinished, glue behind
their eyes loosened by heat, blue gazes rattling

plastic heads, and the priest thinks, *Providence,*
before giving them to me at my mother's funeral.
I dress them in mourning, scold them as I brush

their hair. A capuchin steals one from the cradle
I made out of a plantain crate. The one with
the parted mouth I kiss with the tip of my tongue

until my father gives it away, knowing nothing
of the one I buried after I broke my hymen
on its hand. One was a mermaid's daughter

who drowned, but her body washed up where
a handsome guitarist found her and massaged
her feet until her heart started. I nail one

to a cross as a gift for the priest. I open one
with a kitchen knife to see how girls are made
and rub my finger along the smooth, hollowed

shoulders and hips and thighs. One I dress in mud
and forget it by the river. The tide takes it to a curious
pirarucu, and when the ribereño cuts into his boiled

dinner's belly that night as he argues with his wife
about the last time they made love during a full moon,
a naked plastic girl spills onto his plate, slicked in blood

and fish guts. *Ai Deus!* he cries, but it isn't God at all.
Ai Maria! she cries, which is closer to the miracle
born on their table. A single blue eye crooked

in its socket stares back. The wife grabs a stick
and pushes the hard, unbreathing body back through
the slit in the fish's belly. They'd asked for a son.

At Play in the Fields of the Lord

An electric eel can deliver shocks of 860 volts,
enough to knock a horse off its feet, or kill a woman
washing yellow feathers from her breasts, or stun a god

backstroking through the mangroves. A fact is a thing
of intimacy. A god is mere hypothesis. A mother is
a grief. The rotted body of a horse is a home for an eel.

In Which the Chorus Paints a Family Portrait at Boi Bumbá

MARIA THEREZA

Here's the drunk husband of the dancer singing to the macaw he smuggled into prison.

MARIA HELENA

Here's the wife putting on her costume of a pregnant woman craving a bull's tongue.

MARIA APARECIDA

Here's the never of silence, the yes of an idolizing crowd.

MARIA HELENA

And here's the no in the throat of a woman.

MARIA DE LOURDES

Here's the jaguar that leaped out of the mountain.

MARIA HELENA

And here's the mountain, risking nothing.

MARIA THEREZA

Here's the daughter watching the sky for birds with messages banding their legs. Here she is peeling the costume from her mother's flesh, skin pitted by sequins. Yellow feathers in her hair, her armpits, under her breasts.

MARIA APARECIDA

Here's the mother of a girl washing feathers from her body and into the river, who is the wife of a parrot smuggler but pretending to be the wife of a man who baffled the bull with his strange longing.

MARIA DE LOURDES

Here, at last, is God, the gold plume escaping every mouth.

MARIA HELENA

Here is the daughter again, who sat in the stands, who saw the mountain open, who knew death by its purring.

MARIA THEREZA

Here's the feather still hiding in the crease of thigh and lip.

MARIA MADALENA

Here's the bull, so alive to the shouting.

MARIA HELENA

And here's the look on death's face when it thinks of heaven.

MARIA DE LOURDES

And the rosary in the atheist's pocket.

MARIA THEREZA

And the son who won't be born unfurling his fingers inside his mother standing hip-deep in the river, an eel circling her ankles.

MARIA HELENA

Here's the steadfast desire. The spear.

MARIA APARECIDA

Here's the bull, satisfied at last.

MARIA DE LOURDES

Oh, here's the drum, the drum, the blood returning, the beating, the bull struggling to stand as the wife slices neatly into its cooked tongue.

Revenant

My mother met my father when she fainted after spying
a stain on a barroom floor in the shape of God's left testicle.
When he picked her up, parrots smuggled under his coat flew

from the sleeves. Until the moment she woke in the feathered
arms of such an agreeable savior, her imagination had failed
at joy. At the sight of the birthmark on her forehead, he felt

a bright, unholy hunger. They made love in afternoons,
kissing where the toucans they trafficked had scratched
their calves. After his arrest, she released rare birds over

the prison. He'd watch the sky for hyacinth macaws, banded
cotingas, harpy eagles, living love notes as rare as their story.
Six months pregnant, she killed a jaguar, crawled under its paw,

lifted her chin to its bloodied lip and dreamed God's right testicle
in the shape of a lamb and stirring. Death came as a shadow
on her lung, as gangrene in the stump of her thumb,

as the startled eel at her ankles. My mother of veins blackening
her wrists. My mother of gold carnival mask, of green feathers
sprouting from her shoulders, of glittered body, candled dusk.

Let me inherit her fevered hips. Let me be all wing and stolen
and saved. Mother, rise up as July, as tempest, as God in his night
sweats and be tender. Hold the curtain back while I enter.

What They Found in the Diving Bell

The first time I saw my mother, she'd been dead
fourteen years and came as a ghost in the mirror,
plucking the hair under her arms, and humming

a bossa nova. She lotioned her chapped heels
and padded her bra as if she were alive in the old way.
She said I was born with my cord wrapped

around my neck like a rosary, and she knew God,
the doomed father of her days, wanted us both.
Before midnight she plaited my hair, hemmed

my skirt, sang lullabies she'd learned on the other
side of the flood. She lifted her dress to show
her bones shedding light on a stillborn fetus

accidentally raptured under her ribs. She said
she'd choose her death again, obey any pain
heaven gave her. Years ago she watched a man ride

a diving bell to the bottom of the Amazon to face
the mysteries God placed there. The chain broke,
and they pulled him to the surface smiling, stiff, refusing

to open his fists. They broke and unpeeled his fingers.
No one wept or fought to hold it. She covered her eyes
so she wouldn't see what God, in his innocence, had done.

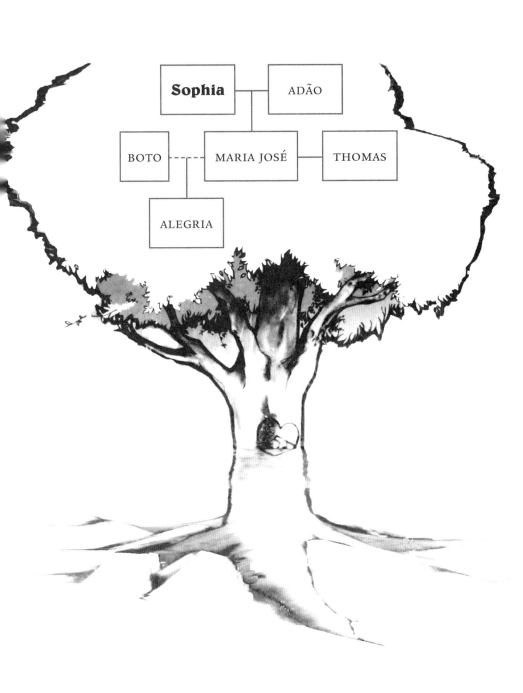

Rapture: *Lucus*

Posters for the missing kapok tree appear on streetlights
offering a reward for its safe return. I hate to spoil it,

but the end of every biography is death. The end of a city
in the rain forest is a legend and a lost expedition. The end

of mythology is forgetfulness, placing gifts in the hole
where the worshipped tree should be. But my memory

lengthens with each ending. I know where to find the lost
mines of Muribeca and how to cross the Pacific on a balsa raft.

I know the tree woke from her stillness one equatorial summer
evening as Adão pulled parrots from her branches.

She dreamed an amorous faun chased her, which was a memory,
which reminded her that in another form she had legs

and didn't need the anxious worship of people who thought
her body was a message. She is happier than the poem

tattooed on her back says she is, but sadder than the parrots
nesting in her hair believed her to be. I am more or less content

to be near her in October storms, though I can't stop thinking
that with the right love or humility or present of silk barrettes

and licorice she might become a myth again in my arms, ardent,
wordless, needing someone to bear her away from the flood.

Ecce Homo, He Says, and I Do

I behold the man chosen — philtrum bristled,
his lip a pink bruise among beard spokes.

The underdown of parakeets nestled
in his armpit, a soft white fury of curls.

He says I'm a better wife than I think I am.
Amorous. Loyal. And I decide to enjoy

the rare comfort of being told I am good,
even as I hide the handcuff key beneath

my tongue. Hair on his chest flat but curving
like a map of the trade winds over his belly.

My love a plummet and a plumbing, a chart
for the nautical miles I travel away and back

again. My love happiest like this, arresting desire
in its nascent swelling. The want lingering in

its catalogue, still sinless and waiting, weighing,
letting imagination tax the body. His knuckles

scarred by the beaks of macaws displeased
at his sweet thieving, splinters in his fingers

from carrying someone else's dream into
the wilderness. One nipple turns in on itself,

the other bitten and unpuckered. The ghost-hoof
arched on his chest like a door to heaven

I could open with a charm, a kiss, a word,
and with a tongue, pull the radiance through.

What We Lost in the Flood —

the barber's best shears, the toucan tucked in Adão's
coat, all the allamanda blossoms, the brown phantom

and his white shadow. The cuckold never came home,
but his pants basked on the courthouse roof for weeks.

Hippolyta sank. The cemetery swelled. The original Christ
above the church vanished along with the toothless nun.

We said: *Our love survived even this.* We believed it. The future
remained waterlogged and when we carved our initials

into the kapok's branches, we felt it dream beneath our knife.
The fateful signature in our blood returned as the thin apostle

of moonlight, as a rooster calling dawn in a caiman's stomach,
as the Pentecostal firing squad, as Senhor Lua's collection —

Divana diva, Papilio achilles, wings pricked by the too late,
the stay away, the not yet delight of tomorrow.

In Which the Chorus Appears
at the Wedding Rehearsal, Ominous as Angels

MARIA HELENA

You quicksilver, you plagiarized prayer infatuated with rain.

MARIA DE LOURDES

You unnecessary virgin disrobing stage right, blushing everywhere but your cheeks.

MARIA APARECIDA

You prudish bride with your unchristian passion, rewriting vows while your nipples stiffen against the lace.

MARIA THEREZA

You unanswerable hypothesis, you too-simple parable, we are unswaddled and reaching for you through the flood season's amnesia, past the love that marked you.

MARIA MADALENA

Past the chain-smoking groom with feathers in his breast pocket and the rum-soaked wedding party, bees feasting in each boutonniere.

MARIA HELENA

Past, past the children making paper planes from the pages of hymnals and the stale destinies of everyone in the first three pews.

MARIA DE LOURDES

To the history before the flood, to the erotic exodus and the purchased sighs.

MARIA APARECIDA

You child of sugarcane, of cardboard and rain, we've been meaning to say: *Not yet, not yet.*

MARIA THEREZA

You're entitled to your miracle, but this isn't it. The hope of this moment will hurt with age.

MARIA HELENA

This moment: the way he looks at you with hooks in his desire.

MARIA MADALENA

Look instead into the red apex of the wound. See what would die for you, what died for you, what's dying for you to reach it.

Virago

No one pays me for sex. They pay to whisper entreaties
to my birthmark of a pink Madonna with her robe open —

the sight of the redeemer's quickening marked with a mole
that swells as I age. I lie there as resigned as a messiah

at his crucifixion while men come with money and troubles
to ask for forgiveness, for mercy, for the secret to finding

the road to El Dorado. They swear she awards them kisses,
sponsors profane intimacies between fireflies and lighthouses.

I used to think God asked this of me — to be still and adored,
let people stare at the benign nevus as though it mirrored

their appetites. I offer every customer a shallow paradise
teeming with eels and as much holy water as they can drink.

I wait on all fours in a white skirt and a conquistador's breastplate
so men must ask me to turn around. My fantasy always accepts me,

even when I try to resist it. When a customer stares at the Virgin
on my forehead, I imagine my hand gripping the sublime manifest

and tumescent. I get more than I deserve but half as much as I want.
Holy Mother, may I put this unchurched man's hands up my shirt?

May I wrap you in bandages and cover him with my body until
we exhaust ourselves with your name? I've grown sick of this numb

obedience, the boring mortal euphoria of men watching you disrobe by my hairline. Sweet Mother, I'd rather be unchosen.

Set me free or I'll veil my forehead. I'll tattoo a machete where your heart should be. O mistress, O miracle, abandon me.

On the Feast Day of Our Lady Hippolyta

I want customers to bring me arrows fletched
with parrot feathers and whisper the password —

sterile — three times before I let them in. I want
men with narrow hips and a good memory for myth

to keep me up all night reading Ovid's *Amores*
or recite Sappho as they groom their mustaches

in the mirror above the bed. I want to bite,
to climb, to zipper my way back into the story where

the Amazon queen appeared in her girdle before
three children and foretold the lumberjack apocalypse.

I want the men who bus in from sapphire mines
and rubber plantations to spend a week's pay on

ten minutes, the sound of their bodies like a fresh
catch slapping the dock, wet and desperate

and piscine, like damp laundry flapping on the line,
like a mule at its branding, like a novitiate visited

by the Holy Spirit in the middle of her vespers.
If I want sonnets to praise the downy hairs on

my upper lip, who cares? If I want to learn about
the French Revolution as I eat cake, so what?

Only on this day does anyone commemorate
children returning home, knees already scabbing

with bark, to warn of bulldozers and chainsaws
and the perils of trees next to power lines. I celebrate

the miracle one customer at a time, nocking
arrows and aiming for the sun's white eye. I want

to write in my diary — *Dear, there are some things
I would not do for pleasure.* I want it to be true.

The Heart in Jeopardy Fabricates a New Fortune

I want you in the worst way, he says, and I don't know
if that means on all fours wearing the rosary I stole

from a nun or on his mother's bed threatening
to punish him, but I say, *Okay,* and start crushing

grapes between my breasts as usual. Earlier today
the Ouija board misspelled its answers, told me,

You are one of the devil's thirteen bridles, and I thought
perhaps I can control him, perhaps the next time

he comes to me I will slip the bit into his mouth
as he licks a lump of sugar from my palm, perhaps,

just once, I will refuse the conjugal untying, the gold
and gloom of his black-tongued ultimatum.

But he brings me yellow velvet shoes, spreads out
photos from his latest investigation and draws

a chalk outline on the floor. *Like this,* he says.
So I do. Necromantic. Prayerful. A willful shadow

crawls up my legs and won't come down. The Ouija
board said, *This is the tie that blinds.* It said, *Never*

tantalize the devil's rock. I hold still as bells publish
the morning light, stiffen as the stolen horses return

from following pleasure to a darker north, carrying
canting executioners on their backs and the blackest joy.

Reluctant Fugue

I will burn down the trees engraved with poems,
ignite miscarried lines and deflowered stanzas,

cauterize couplets about pirates named after apostles
who terrorized the river — Matthew the silver thief;

Mark the rubber-seed smuggler; Luke the kidnapper
of accordions; John, who liberated dresses

from widows and sketched them, amazed and gazing
at his stigmata, in quaking peach slips. The words

carved in the trees confess everything, bold as hyacinth macaws
colonizing the branches advertising remorseless saviors

lurking in the undergrowth. I'll destroy graffitied trees
bearing the nights and sorrows of a city. I'll raze the leaves

so no one ever learns what I learned when I woke from
my fugue with a butterfly knife and saw my hand finishing

my dream's ecclesiastic work. I'll keep them from knowing
we're the authors of our own unknowns, worriers puzzling trees

with immortal longing. I'll protect the wonder, cut down
scarred limbs and turn them into telegraph poles christened

with *Prayer,* into cradles that read *Requiescat,* into coffins saying,
Carry me to Penuel, into statues of saints whittled with *Fire.*

In Which the Chorus Whispers the Rumors

MARIA APARECIDA

The oracle has been seen riding a Victoria lily pad holding up seven fingers. She's nearly ready to be born again.

MARIA HELENA

Ribereños say the ichor in her veins lights up at night, as in the dark origin of the word.

MARIA THEREZA

Her tongue swells until she reaches the confluence of the Rio Negro's black waters and the muddy Amazon and begins to speak in *we*.

MARIA DE LOURDES

As in all of us.

MARIA MADALENA

As in all lost children.

MARIA APARECIDA

As in the boy born from a tree who's irresistible to birds. As in the daughter with her father most of all. As in follow them, follow them. And we do.

MARIA HELENA

Her beauty pleases the part of us that gazes.

MARIA THEREZA

Her words feed the part that longs to hear our secrets in someone else's mouth.

Holding our breath, we brush away mosquitoes whining above us,
and then she tells us everything—

MARIA MADALENA

Jemimah, Keziah, Keren-Happuch. Soon. Soon. What has been taken
will be replaced and newly named.

The Unverifiable Resurrection of Adão da Barco

First, a tourist finds a word scarring a kapok
in the leper colony, ants swarming sap in the cuts.

Then a fisherman uncovers instructions for a rain dance,
an usher discovers recipes for the jubilee.

A riverboat captain comes to town and leads us
to a tree in the north describing the mating habits

of the marabunta, to one in the south with a sonnet
about a hen named Lucifer whose fiendish eggs buzzed.

No one believes the boy he carries off the boat is his own,
not even when he shows them the statue of the sundered

Madonna whose toothsome breasts smell like the common,
vulgar sweetness of maracujá. But I never saw the boy

in his first life, birth-wet and trying to fly. I saw the mule,
wasp-stung and raging, trample him in front of an elegy

for Lazarus's wife. I collected mummified hummingbirds
for his pockets, a wishbone for the reddening hoof

on his chest. His father returned from the jungle with
something dripping from his knife – pulsing, doubtless,

radiant. What could bring back a son. What in God's name
was sweet, is sweet, will be sweeter after sundering.

After the Flood the Captain
of the *Hamadryas* Discovers a Madonna

He pulled everything he could save out of the water —
canoes snarled in tree roots, bruised mangoes,

cans of chilies, crates and crates of plantains splitting
from their tough yellowed skins — before he found her

upside down in a cecropia robed in mud and fish bones,
a woman's floral underwear wrapped around her feet.

He wiped the dirt from between her lips with a callused thumb
and felt what he dreaded — a god-awful abundance of wonder.

Town after town, he towed the Mother of God, but no one
would take her. One town said it lost a Christ with paint

flaking from his face. Another said they lost cattle to the river.
Another, a child. He offered the blooming peony panties

to every shaking head. For weeks, he rowed through storm
and sunstroke, promised her, *To God, the glory. To God, the power.*

To you the devotion of a penitent thief. But she remained unclaimed.
Macaws landed on her shoulders and sang whale songs.

When he cupped her smaller breast, he heard bells tolling
his own name. Morphos cloaked her at dusk, mated on her back

or slipped their proboscises, deep and tenderly, beneath her
blistered paint for the sweetness seeping from her warped hips.

One night as he passed a boat where men laughed as they threw
rotting fish at caimans, her peeling cheeks smoothed, her splinters

lay back into the wood, her belly rounded against the robe, the child
inside turning as it dreamed its own heartbeat. Then, he saw.

Then, he sorrowed. Then, the shameless, mortal awe as he cried,
For thine is the kingdom, and rolled up his sleeves to deliver her.

Misbegotten

My father is made of gold and my mother is a dryad
with pomegranates in her hair and a peach pit for a heart.

Or my father is a mime in the night circus and my mother
sings the dark circles from his eyes. Or my mother sang

and my father loved and forgot he had a wife. I am orphic
am ophidian am orphan. When I swim the mangroves,

snakes climb my legs for refuge. I stretch the dead from
tongue to tail, shape six silhouettes of my body and name

them all sister, trade my stolen Bible for romance novels
and dry myself with the pages. The lost have a paradise, too.

The first naked man I saw was dead. His body summoned
only indifference, his sex soft in his lap, a threat to no one.

It is humiliating to love a dead woman more than the father
who braids orchids into your hair, and yet — I survive

the same lie twice, coax the serpent's forked heart
to ring the bells lonelier than elegies, *gone, gone, gone.*

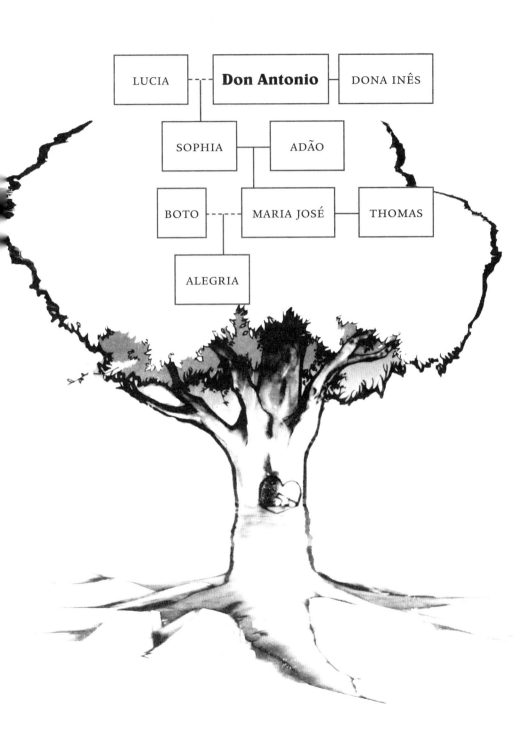

Sibylline Translation

Emergency, I'll be your siren. Imagination, I'll be your figment.
    Fiction is one way of knowing. Dreams are another.
Meanwhile, the dead trample the psalmic grass as they line up
    to ride bald angels like horses through the graveyard.
Lazarused but not yet rising, their bodies crowd the fence
    waiting for news of the hereafter while the undertaker collects
a toll from pallbearers. Blame the congregation tithing
    wisdom teeth, or the moon which has been full for weeks.
Lunacy, I'm already yours. I made my truth. Consequence,
    I'll be your whipping boy, your pulled hair and burning nerve.
My wife left me. She has no grave. But my mistress is waiting,
    an aria trapped in her throat that will tell me what I am.
I will suck rust from the nails holding down her casket lid. Out
    of her whitening mouth, a bright nothing will aerialize, ascend.

Plantation Landscape with Seven Unwanted Children and Pollinating Rubber Trees

Little knights, little queens, little overseers
    of this squalid kingdom. One is my daughter
but I never know which. In the dry season
    the river retreats, and rocks reveal the faces
of everyone who's gone missing since rubber
    seeds were smuggled out of the jungle. Not all
love stories endure. I know; I buried one.
    I kissed her body as it grew cold and then bit
her lip to see whether she would still bleed for me.
    Some loves leave you, and some stay and waste,
some sweat while you trim their fingernails and nick
    the soft meat of their thumbs, some depart
in the middle of your endearments and rush into
    a darkness you cannot fathom or follow.
But these little tyrants last and last. They rub the stones'
    faces with coal over paper. It's like grief
but as innocent as they are. They hang their grave
    rubbings from rubber trees that weep white sap
on the dates. Sometimes I hear the rubber seeds land
    on the rain-forest floor, hear them rooting, hear
their ambitious fertility push into the crowded dirt.
    The little rioters burn my Victrola, deface
my sheet music with hearts and stars, cut up
    my maps and replace all the sea monsters
with missionaries in large black robes. I tell them lies
    with enough truth to satisfy. *Love yourself,* I say.
Marry your enemy. They ruin religiously, singing
    tedious songs as they unbraid my whips
with all the tenderness they once must have known.

Il dolce suono

Ghosts of contraltos orbit the equator, blinking,
    every message the same. *The holy torches are shining,*
shining. The dead are more real than the children
    making me paper crowns, who remember nothing
of the bite, the burn, the fever, the benign power
    of health. I cut the blindfold from my daughter
to see whether her pupils hold the forecast of whatever
    black light will come for her, but the spirit refuses
to pass itself off as an image. History is more real
    than the sticky peppermints placed in my palm
by a child who does not know I once owned this land
    and everyone on it. The future comes for me even
as I reenact the past with the ghosts in my attic. They aria,
    I applaud. They cadenza, they coloratura, I adore.
Breath escapes, then memory. Then God permits the dead
    to visit — *Ah, quella voce* — so I can try to lick
the music out of her mouth and she sings — *Let us take*
    refuge here, it is scattered with roses — to the child
who remembers nothing, not even the love that made her.

Translation Theory

I thought *possession,* when you said the simile
    was the rhetorical tool of the colonial encounter,
like pulling a psalm from a tree with forceps.
    Thought *awe,* like my God but without a crown
and fewer horses. Thought *recorder,* remember,
    from the Latin *re-cordis,* to pass back through
the heart. Dined on songbirds and imported wine
    and thought, *their gods would've surrendered to me*
if I were taller. Thought *gold,* thought *land,* thought *dear subjects.*
    Thought *control,* like a groom tattooing his *I do*
on his bride's thigh, like the bride transcribing a groom's vows
    in chalk, like the merchant peddling chalk and needles.
I thought the evidence of love was in the suffering.
    Thought, *die for me,* like imagination's darkest figment.
Thought *glory,* like the captive with wrists bound
    singing black vowels into the gun's barrel. The word
transubstantiated into the machine, wonderful in its throb.
    The heart, that divine assailant. What's pulled
from the earth but not translated — the mud and the red
    of it, the blood and the wet of it.

Matar as Saudades

In the short dream, she falls down the stairs again and again,
    singing in a bloodied wedding dress, the crowd
breathless. My hands tied, again, to the chair to keep me from
    rushing the stage and kissing her lovely, dead mouth.
I never wanted her more than when she died for a love she
    pretended was real. Desire's sweetest fiction in three acts
and an encore. In the middle dream, an angel milks venom
    from a snake while I dig and dig in the wet dirt of a grave
to pull free a child. Waxy thing, unwelcome need, forehead
    stained with pink. The child's birthmark —
her mother's silhouette. I command my beloved to return
    to me but the child wails and wails, weeping white sap
until my hands stick to her. A contract. The will of the forest.
    A love with a future instead of a past. Like glass shattered
by a high note, it is foreshadowed by music. Like a dog
    bristling between a girl and a jaguar, it is ferocious
and sleepless and bound for tragedy, but not now. Now begins
    the long dream where I believe my fear and adore it,
where I hear a song I lived in my early years, pealing
    underwater like a summons. It belongs to a longing
that murmured my name before falling down a flight of stairs,
    that I still seek knowing I'll find snakes nesting
in the rotted house and the dear dead on my old mattress,
    her mouth bloodless, waiting, impossible, oh, resist.

Belterra Exodus

When the miracles return and demand their price,
    I pawn my cameo with the silhouette of a kraken,
whistle the children away with the soft magic of magnets
    I drop like breadcrumbs to lead them to the abandoned
plantation where spirits don't break loose and a body needs
    a mind to animate it — none of the flawed transcendence
plaguing this town with eels teeming in swimming pools.
    The children march two by two, such sweet order.
They take so little convincing. Dirty cubs. Hungry cherubs.
    Fear not, I say, *the American plantation. They returned north
and took their square dancing with them.* It is a place without
    blessings, and therefore safe. The rubber trees stopped
their white weeping, therefore fear not the footprints
    in the mud. We should give ourselves over to wishes,
which are all imagination and no faith. We should invent a new
    history of fact and fancy, where life is hard but courage
is easy because the dead do not resurrect themselves and claim
    to be beloved, and the dead do not write their names
on trees, and the dead do not crawl out of the river looking
    for their eyes. And they will love me. They will.
With the kind of romantic suffering I was promised.
    Here, we will trace our shadows in dirt, and here
we will wrinkle and weaken and wait. Here, God will question
    his own Heaven, his zealous investment in eternity.
Here his bosom will be supple and sweet, and he will hold us
    to it until we stop struggling with the temptation to live
and feel a love so perfect it asks for its breath back and we give it.

After Seven Lullabies Vanish from the Library

In a bullet-riddled villa my filha and I choreograph sword fights
    and sing to militant termites feasting on the walls.
We read newspapers from headlines to horoscope.
    Our nights too long. Our bed too big for every room.
We turn invisible doorknobs, light ignis fatuus chandeliers.
    We paint the storyteller's body when she loses her voice,
and we pass her around a circle, naming what we see —
    Myrmidons! Saturn! — a storm flickering in the god's eye.
On her hip, the ascendant unborn. A tooth-white thigh
    engraved with handprints. An arm of starfall
in daylight. I warn her it will be a small story, a smaller
    house, the smallest mermaid's purse preserved in a jar.
Sometimes my daughter looks so much like her mother
    I want to barter with Heaven. It took the wrong love.
Era uma vez… Lightning on the Atlantic looking for trees.
    A nautilus moaning a monody. There is no ending
to be had. Sleep kisses our eyelids. Stars wheel in the dreams.
    The river plants its tide in us, saying, *sea, sea, sea.*

In Which the Chorus Relates the Somewhat
True History of Puraquequara

MARIA HELENA

On Saturday nights everyone gathers in the rooster graveyard to reenact the town's founding.

MARIA MADALENA

We wear pineapple headdresses and inside-out nightgowns while counting off Paz, Baptista, Lua, Souza, Da Silva, Da Ouro, pretending to be daughters of the founding fathers who fled sapphire mines upriver in search of a place where each could find his one, his only, his starstruck beloved and shudder with her in the open air.

MARIA DE LOURDES

The miners swam with chests of cayenne pepper and chicken eggs on their heads seeking a mythical tribe of one-breasted warriors.

MARIA THEREZA

Instead they met a swarm of eels who morphed into women wearing electric dresses that slid to their waists as the men asked *What is this place, who are you, may I touch you here,* trembled, and opened their eyes to find their brides gone, their children in their arms, and a word carved into a tree.

MARIA APARECIDA

Now, chaperoned by a priest picking the scabs of his stigmata, we walk clockwise around the statue of Barcelos, and boys sting their lips with wasps before circling.

MARIA HELENA

When an arrangement of grapes, guavas, and ripe bananas catches his eye, a boy will ask us a riddle.

MARIA MADALENA

If we answer correctly, we can stroll to the edges of the gravestones so he may confess his love of thick earlobes.

MARIA DE LOURDES

If we answer incorrectly, he must scratch the grass looking for worms.

MARIA THEREZA

When one of us notices a boy's pouting lips and flushed eyelids, we stake our headdress on the granite rooster's spur and offer the weeping boy a wax star fruit.

MARIA APARECIDA

We'll leave the turning of our brothers and sisters to steal pastéis from the bakery and eat in the alley with plastic spoons.

MARIA HELENA

We'll soothe the boy's fevered lips as hormones loosen our hips and the capillaries in our cheeks.

MARIA MADALENA

He'll swear to build a city when he grows up where all lovers will have careers in pleasure, and eggs will bring forth rum and menthol cigarettes while we undress asking *Do you want to, are you ready, does that hurt,* before we see a hand writing on the wall, before it picks the crushed acai from our hair, before it marks the boy's chest with an X, before we are found, sated, beneath the word pulled from us like a rib.

The Hunger River

It was named long before I shot my horse for trying
    to follow me, but that's all anyone remembers —
how I went mad when my beloved died.
    Even though I nursed her through yellow fever,
my body remained strong enough to carry her to the grave.
    I used to bring her orchids and ripe maracujá.
She'd sing private arias in her dressing room while
    I kissed the inside of her knees. I'd rest my cheek
on the hairs of her calf, close my eyes, and hear
    each note travel down her chest, round her hips,
and roll through her legs to my waiting ear. A crooked
    crescent-moon scar carved itself on her left patella
one night when she snagged her skin on an exposed nail
    during a performance. As she stumbled and cried out,
the audience, believing it was grief that crippled her,
    wept harder. After they buried her in a Lucia costume,
I fed my horses champagne, set fire to my villa, and rowed
    out alone to the hunger river. One horse got free
of the fire and followed from shore. When the trees began
    to thicken, it jumped in and swam behind me
as I raved — *I surrender to you! I have escaped from your enemies* —
    but the horse did not turn back, even when
I took out my gun. *Adoration is awful,* I thought. Water rushed
    through the bullet hole and into the skull like
a blessing. The horse's skeleton can still be found —
    white, impossibly radiant, aspiring to immortality
at the bottom of the river. An eel made its home
    in the ribcage, flicking its black tail between the bones.

Idyll, or Impossible Epithalamium

We know the end is near. Rumors reach us
    of the seeds smuggled, and other rubber barons
begin hoisting their grand pianos on steamboats,
    loading their opera glasses and linen suits in trunks.
But our story's conclusion seems so far away in these afternoons
    when I sell taxidermied piranhas to tourists while
she steals beauty magazines from the drugstore. Our fantasies
    are not wishes, but sometimes as she sleeps I measure her
for a wedding dress. Sometimes I wake and find valentines
    on my chest. I pick a maracujá for her, she picks a jambu
for me, and we pretend love is this simple, that make-believe
    equals anonymity equals romance. We swear
we belong only to each other and invent our futures. A future
    of children and Atlantic seas, a future of oracles and flights,
of mysteries naming themselves, of infinite pink seductions.
    Even an arrogant imagination runs out of fantasy,
but for now our story is in its second act and building.
    For now, I remain her afternoon samba. She stays
my sweet disobedience, my happily, my ever, my soon.

In Which the Chorus Tries to Be as Clear as Possible

MARIA DE LOURDES

The past, that is known.

MARIA MADALENA

Once upon a glory, a continent of lumber, rubber, and oil.

MARIA APARECIDA

Once upon a century, heroes.

MARIA HELENA

Once upon a millennium past, wilderness.

MARIA THEREZA

It is a story made of fragments and quartzdust.

MARIA DE LOURDES

History of apologies and peep shows. Record on a Victrola skipping on the same crescendo every time.

MARIA MADALENA

There is no fairy tale here to invite you to meaning, only the fantasy of the past you made in your own image.

MARIA APARECIDA

It's the language of tough and shuffle, of rain-forest striptease and concrete migraines.

MARIA HELENA

It's the song a father sings to the child who followed him into the wilderness.

It's the submission to the sweet reason of the spirit, which is love, which is the reaching back and shedding memory for heartbeats.

MARIA DE LOURDES

For revise, erase, rewrite, alone, astound.

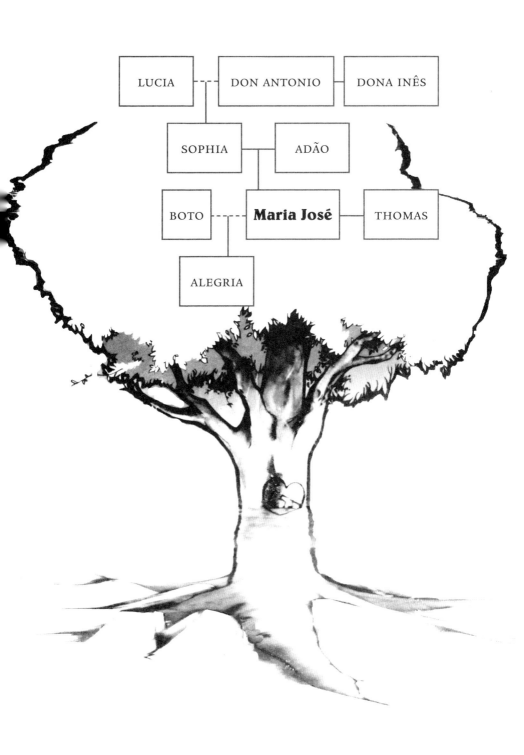

Saudade

Each time I start, the explorers and tyrants,
encantados and daughters are already dead. If you want
to know what I long for, I'd say a world of my own

making where changing destinies is a phrase away,
where everything is true but retreats when you try
to touch it. Where saintless miracles frequent

because the awe is boundless and the drink specials
are cheap. Where I am capable of a quieter greatness
and can write the story I wish someone had written

for me. If only the past would have me now that I have
its answers — its griefs and inheritances. I've given
at least half my faith to madness, the rest

to the chapters written for those who were made
for more loneliness. Not this present with its
halfhearted daydreams and migrating graves.

You can grieve something you've never seen.
The past seems more sure, more endless. Time
moves, but I won't. I will wait for the what-was

to return, the way it did once, that morning
I found a naked girl in my field, her body sure
as prose. When I reached, her flesh vanished,

her bones lay white as paper. My hand, all urge
and no sentiment, bled into her ribs, joyful,
beholding, waiting for the word to begin.

About the Author

Traci Brimhall is the author of *Our Lady of the Ruins* (W.W. Norton), winner of the Barnard Women Poets Prize, and *Rookery* (Southern Illinois University Press), winner of the Crab Orchard Series in Poetry First Book Award. Her poems have appeared in *The Believer, Best American Poetry* (2013 and 2014), *Kenyon Review, New Republic, The New Yorker, Ploughshares, Poetry,* and *Slate,* among other publications. She has received fellowships from the Wisconsin Institute for Creative Writing and the National Endowment for the Arts. She's an assistant professor of Creative Writing at Kansas State University and lives in Manhattan, Kansas.

Poetry is vital to language and living. Since 1972, Copper Canyon Press has published extraordinary poetry from around the world to engage the imaginations and intellects of readers, writers, booksellers, librarians, teachers, students, and donors.

WE ARE GRATEFUL FOR THE MAJOR SUPPORT PROVIDED BY:

THE PAUL G. ALLEN
FAMILY FOUNDATION

Anonymous

Jill Baker and Jeffrey Bishop

Donna and Matt Bellew

John Branch

Diana Broze

Sarah and Tim Cavanaugh

Janet and Les Cox

Mimi Gardner Gates

Linda Gerrard and Walter Parsons

Gull Industries, Inc.
on behalf of Ruth and William True

The Trust of Warren A. Gummow

Steven Myron Holl

Phil Kovacevich and Eric Wechsler

Lakeside Industries, Inc.
on behalf of Jeanne Marie Lee

TO LEARN MORE ABOUT UNDERWRITING
COPPER CANYON PRESS TITLES,
PLEASE CALL 360-385-4925 EXT. 103

WE ARE GRATEFUL FOR THE MAJOR SUPPORT PROVIDED BY:

Maureen Lee and Mark Busto
Rhoady Lee and Alan Gartenhaus
Ellie Mathews and Carl Youngmann as The North Press
Anne O'Donnell and John Phillips
Petunia Charitable Fund and advisor Elizabeth Hebert
Suzie Rapp and Mark Hamilton
Joseph C. Roberts
Jill and Bill Ruckelshaus
Cynthia Lovelace Sears and Frank Buxton
Kim and Jeff Seely
Catherine Eaton Skinner and David Skinner
Dan Waggoner
Austin Walters
Barbara and Charles Wright
The dedicated interns and faithful volunteers
of Copper Canyon Press

The Chinese character for poetry is made up of two parts: "word" and "temple." It also serves as pressmark for Copper Canyon Press.

This book is set in Legacy, designed by Ronald Arnholm.
The display type is set in Belwe, designed by Georg Belwe.
Book design by VJB/Scribe. Printed on archival-quality paper.